A Little

WINE

Printed in the United States of America
by G&R Publishing Co.

Distributed By:

507 Industrial Street
Waverly, IA 50677

ISBN-13: 978-1-56383-215-4
ISBN-10: 1-56383-215-1
Item #6201

Every year, each grape from every branch in all the vineyards across the world has a chance to mark its individual name in the world of wine. The subtle differences in these variables create a never ending, continuously changing, vastly growing wine industry, full of curious tasters, shy beginners, masterful palates and, the infamous, wine snob.

It was not that long ago in America that wine was a rare and expensive addition to the dinner table – a sort of delicacy. In recent decades, however, the American appreciation for wine has undergone a veritable revolution. The country has welcomed the many variations and flavors of wine with open arms and has created an

CABERNET SAUVIGNON
Vin de Pays d'Oc
1999   750 ml

environment where the sweet drink is now included in everyday life. Wine lists are a common sight at restaurants and fine dining cafes and wine is often the beverage of choice for celebrations of all types.

Champagne is synonymous with merry making, Merlot is respected and mature, while Riesling is perfect for that sweet occasion. Zinfandel is fruity, Port is confident, Pinot Noir is complex, Chardonnay is rich, Grenache is hearty and Cabernet is the king. Intrigued? Well, choose your varietal, carefully uncork the bottle, pour the fragrant beverage into your glass and savor the taste before turning the page to learn more about the vast world of wine…

HOT SPICED WINE

Makes 8 to 10 servings

1 liter red wine
½ liter water
½ vanilla bean
½ cinnamon stick
2 tsp. grated orange peel

1 tsp. grated lemon peel
20 cloves
3 hibiscus flowers
Sugar to taste

In a large saucepan or pot over medium heat, combine red wine, water, vanilla bean, cinnamon stick, grated orange peel, grated lemon peel, cloves and flowers. Mix lightly and bring to a boil. Add sugar to taste. Reduce heat and cook for an additional 10 minutes. Before serving, remove spices, orange peel and lemon peel. Ladle spiced wine into mugs.

PASSION FRUIT PUNCH
Makes 65 (6 oz.) servings

1 (25 oz.) bottle Mead*
1 (28 oz.) bottle passion
   fruit juice
2 (64 oz.) bottles orange
   juice
2 (46 oz.) cans unsweetened
   pineapple juice

6 oz. grenadine syrup
2 (8 oz.) bottles lime juice
8 (32) oz. bottles ginger ale

In a large punch bowl, combine Mead, passion fruit juice, orange juice and pineapple juice. Mix lightly and stir in grenadine, lime juice and ginger ale. To serve, ladle punch into glasses. If desired, recipe can easily be cut in half or doubled.

*Mead is a honey wine that is generally fruity and light yellow in color.

SIMPLE WINE COOLER
Makes 1 serving

¾ C. to 1 C. blush wine　　**¼ C. Sprite soda**
¼ C. lemonade

Chill all ingredients in refrigerator. To prepare, in a cocktail shaker filled with ice, combine blush wine, lemonade and Sprite. Shake vigorously and strain into a tall glass. If desired, add ice to glass.

BLACKBERRY SANGRIA
Makes 35 (6 oz.) servings

1 gallon port blackberry wine	½ C. brandy
1 qt. orange juice	½ C. sugar
1 C. lemon juice	1 qt. club soda

Chill all ingredients in refrigerator. In a large punch bowl, combine blackberry wine, orange juice, lemon juice, brandy and sugar. Before serving, add club soda and stir until well mixed. To serve, ladle punch into glasses.

FROM GRAPE TO CUP IN 6 STEPS

The natural process of fermenting grapes and grape juice into wine has taken place for thousands of years. During the process, there are numerous choices that will affect the final taste and quality of the wine. Below are the six steps that almost all grapes endure before making their way to the wine glass.

ONE – HARVESTING

Picking the fruit is the first step to creating wine. Grapes are the most reliable fruit for making wine, as they produce a consistent amount of sugar, helping to yield sufficient alcohol to preserve the resulting beverage. Determining when the grapes are ready for harvest is done by many scientific methods, as well as old-fashioned grape tasting. Harvesting can be done mechanically or by hand, though many vineyards prefer to hand harvest, as mechanical harvesters can often be too rough on the grapes and the vineyard. When the grapes arrive at the winery, they are sorted into bunches and rotten or under ripe fruit are removed.

TWO – CRUSHING

For thousands of years, crushing was traditionally performed by placing whole clusters of grapes in huge barrels. Men and women would perform the "harvest dance" by stomping over the grapes to burst the sweet grape juice from the skins. Today, mechanical crushers perform this process, eliminating the romance of the harvest crushing celebration. However, the mechanical process is much more sanitary and has improved the longevity and quality of wine while also eliminating the need for added preservatives. Some winemakers choose not to crush the grapes at all, allowing the natural weight of the grapes and the fermentation process to burst the skins before pressing the uncrushed clusters.

THREE – PRESSING

Up until the pressing process, the steps for making white wine and red wine are basically the same. If a winemaker is producing white

11

W I N E

wine, he will quickly press the crushed grapes in order to separate the skins and seeds from the juice. White wine is allowed very little time in contact with the grape skins, which determine the color of the liquid. By quickly removing the skins, any unwanted color and tannins cannot make their way into the white wine. On the other hand, red wine is left in contact with its grape skins for a longer period of time in order to pull color, flavor and additional tannins from the grapes.

FOUR – FERMENTATION

The magical process of fermenting crushed grapes into wine is done both naturally and purposely. Crushed grapes and juice will begin to ferment naturally within 6 to 12 hours with the help of wild yeasts in the air. However, many winemakers choose to kill the wild and natural yeasts and introduce a more predictable yeast in order to more readily determine the end result. Either way, once fermentation begins, it normally continues until all of the sugar from the grapes has been converted to alcohol and a dry wine remains. This process can last anywhere from 10 days to a couple months. To produce a sweeter wine, the fermenting process is stopped before all of the sugar has been converted into alcohol.

FIVE – CLARIFICATION

Once fermentation is complete, winemakers choose how many solids they wish to remove from the wine. The alcohol is often siphoned from one tank or barrel to another in order to remove all wine, leaving the solids, known as the pomace, in the bottom of the fermenting tank. Some winemakers will filter or fin their wine to determine clarification. Filtering can be either simple or precise, with wine makers using everything from course filters to catch only large solids to sterile filter pads, which remove nearly every bit of pomace. Fining occurs when substances are added in order to clarify the wine. Compounds, such as clay or egg whites, are often added to adhere to unwanted solids, forcing them to the bottom of the tank. The clarified wine is then transferred to another tank.

SIX – FINISHING

Finishing involves the aging and bottling of the wine. The winemaker chooses to either bottle the wine immediately or to give the wine additional aging. It is at this step that winemakers employ personal techniques, which are nearly endless, in order to determine the end result of the wine.

ORANGE COOLER
Makes 1 serving

¾ C. orange wine   ¼ C. lemon-lime soda
½ C. orange juice

Chill all ingredients in refrigerator. To prepare, in a cocktail shaker filled with ice, combine orange wine and orange juice. Shake vigorously and strain into a tall glass.
Add lemon-lime soda and stir lightly. If desired, add ice
to glass.

"*Here's to the corkscrew –*
a useful key to unlock
the storehouse of wit, the
treasury of laughter, the
front door of fellowship and
the gate of pleasant folly."

W.E.P. French

RED WINE LEMON PUNCH
Makes 22 (4 oz.) servings

3 (6 oz.) cans frozen pink lemonade concentrate, divided
1 (10 oz.) jar maraschino cherries
1 (2 liter) bottle lemon-lime soda
1 (750 ml.) bottle red wine
1 orange, sliced
1 lemon, sliced

In a large pitcher, combine 1 can pink lemonade concentrate and 1 can water. Mix well and pour mixture into an ice cube tray. Place one cherry in each cube and place in freezer until solid. In a large punch bowl, combine remaining 2 cans pink lemonade concentrate, lemon-lime soda and red wine. Mix well and stir in frozen lemonade ice cubes. Garnish punch bowl with remaining cherries, orange slices and lemon slices. To serve, ladle into punch glasses.

HAWAIIAN WINE PUNCH
Makes 24 (6 oz.) servings

1 (46 oz.) can Hawaiian
   fruit punch
¼ C. sugar
½ C. brandy

1 (25 oz.) bottle
   strawberry wine
2 (1 qt.) bottles
   lemon-lime soda

Chill all ingredients in refrigerator. In a large punch bowl, combine Hawaiian fruit punch, sugar, brandy and strawberry wine. Before serving, add lemon-lime soda and stir until well mixed. To serve, ladle punch into glasses.

BASIC SANGRIA
Makes 8 servings

1 orange
2 limes
1 C. fresh chopped
  pineapple
1 C. pitted and halved
  cherries

1 (750 ml.) bottle red
  wine
1 liter lemon-lime soda

Slice orange and limes into thin slices and place in a punch bowl. Add chopped pineapple and cherries. Add red wine and mix lightly. Slowly pour in lemon-lime soda to taste. Taste after adding half of the lemon-lime soda, being careful not to over-dilute the wine. To serve, ladle sangria into punch glasses and garnish each serving with some of the fruit pieces.

PINA COLADA

Makes 6 servings

1 lemon
1 T. sugar
4 sliced pineapple rings

1 (750 ml.) bottle
   white wine
2 C. lemon-lime soda

Thoroughly wash lemon and cut into thin slices. Place lemon slices in a one gallon jar and add sugar. Cut pineapple into very fine pieces and add to jar. Add white wine and lemon-lime soda. Mix well, cover jar and refrigerate for 2 hours. To serve, strain mixture into glasses.

THE TEST OF TIME

Wine was one of the first things man created on earth, though no one knows the exact origin of the drink. More than almost any other product, wine has woven its way through human history, playing roles in religious ceremonies, as medicine and antiseptic, as a water purifier and as a comforting friend. Below are just a few historical references and occurrences that prove the early production and consumption of wine:

- The Old Testament of the Bible
- Greek & Roman mythology
- Written Egyptian references dating back to 5000 BC

- The planting of vineyards around 1000 BC in Italy and Northern Africa
- 16th century explorers transporting wine to Mexico and Japan
- Around 1560, Argentina and Peru imported vine plantings
- Planting of vineyards in 1697 in what is known today as California

"*I love everything that's old: old friends, old times, old manners, old books, old wines.*"

Oliver Goldsmith

FIZZY STRAWBERRY WINE PUNCH
Makes 15 (6 oz.) servings

1 C. sugar
½ C. water
2 C. strawberry wine
2 C. orange juice

½ C. lemon juice
1 C. crushed fresh or frozen strawberries
1 qt. club soda

In a small saucepan over medium heat, combine sugar and water. Meanwhile, chill remaining ingredients in refrigerator. Bring sugar mixture to a boil, stirring constantly, until a syrup forms. Remove from heat and let cool. In a large punch bowl, combine strawberry wine, orange juice, lemon juice and crushed strawberries and cooled syrup mixture. Before serving, add club soda and mix lightly.

CHERRY COLA COOLER

Makes 1 serving

1 C. cherry wine   **1 maraschino cherry**
1 C. cola

In a cocktail shaker filled with ice, combine cherry wine and cola. Shake well and strain mixture into a tall glass. If desired, add ice and garnish with a cherry.

CHAMPAGNE PUNCH
Makes 35 (4 oz.) servings

1 (12 oz.) can frozen cranberry juice concentrate

1 (12 oz.) can frozen pink
lemonade concentrate

1 (6 oz.) can frozen limeade
concentrate

1 (750 ml.) bottle white
wine, chilled

1 liter club soda, chilled

2 (750 ml.) bottles
Champagne, chilled

1 lemon, sliced

½ C. fresh mint sprigs

In a large punch bowl, combine cranberry juice concentrate, pink lemonade concentrate, limeade concentrate,
white wine, club soda and Champagne. Mix lightly and
garnish bowl with lemon slices. To serve, ladle into punch
glasses and garnish each glass with a sprig of fresh mint.

Burgundy makes you think of silly things, Bordeaux makes you talk of them and Champagne makes you do them.

Jean-Anthelme Brillat-Savarin

CAROLING WINE

Makes 8 servings

1 C. water
1 C. brown sugar
2 C. pineapple juice
1 C. orange juice
6 whole cloves
3 whole allspice berries

10 cinnamon sticks,
 divided
½ tsp. salt
2 oranges
4 C. red wine

In a large saucepan over medium heat, combine water, brown sugar, pineapple juice and orange juice. Mix lightly and add whole cloves, whole allspice berries, 2 cinnamon sticks and salt. Cut the peel of the oranges into strips and add to the mixture. Bring mixture to a boil, stirring occasionally, reduce heat and let simmer for 15 minutes. Add wine, bring to a boil and remove from heat. To serve, ladle hot drink into 8 mugs and garnish each mug with one of the remaining cinnamon sticks.

LEMON EGGNOG

Makes 20 servings

4 egg whites	1 C. honey
1 oz. white wine	6 C. milk
½ C. fresh lemon juice	1 qt. half n' half
1 T. grated lemon peel	Pinch of nutmeg

In a medium bowl, using a wire whisk, beat egg whites until stiff peaks form and set aside. In a large saucepan over medium heat, combine wine, lemon juice, grated lemon peel and honey. Heat, stirring constantly, until warmed. Slowly add milk and half n' half and continue to cook, stirring until mixture is frothy. Remove from heat and fold in egg whites. Divide mixture evenly into mugs and garnish each serving with a sprinkle of nutmeg.

FLAVORFUL FRUITS

Most wine is derived from the juice of grapes, however, the general term for wine refers to the natural fermented juice of any fresh fruit or berry. Though grapes are the preferred wine-making fruit, there are many "country wines" made from other fruits, vegetables, seeds, grains, leaves, flowers, bark, roots and other non-grape ingredients, such as:

- Strawberries
- Guava fruit
- Cherries
- Dandelions
- Cranberries
- Pears
- Lemon
- Raisins
- Tomatoes
- Pineapple

- Raspberries
- Turnips
- Blackberries
- Apples
- Carrots
- Mango
- Lime
- Rhubarb
- Wheat
- Elderberries

"*So life's year begins and closes;*

Days though shortening still can shine;

What though youth gave love and roses;

Age still leaves us friends and wine."

Thomas Moore

AFTER SNOW HOT COCKTAIL
Makes 6 (4 oz.) servings

¾ C. water	1 orange
¾ C. sugar	10 whole cloves
1 cinnamon stick	1 (750 ml.) bottle red wine

In a large saucepan over medium heat, combine water, sugar and cinnamon stick. Bring to a boil, reduce heat and let simmer. Meanwhile, cut the orange in half and squeeze the juice from both halves into the mixture. Push the whole cloves into the outside of the orange peel and add to mixture. Simmer for 30 minutes, until mixture is thickened and syrupy. Add wine and continue heating, being careful not to let mixture simmer. Remove oranges and ladle hot mixture into mugs.

BISSCHOPSWIJN
(meaning Bishop's wine in Dutch)

1 (750 ml.) bottle red wine   **1 orange**
½ C. sugar   **8 whole cloves**
1 tsp. cinnamon

In a large saucepan over medium low heat, combine red wine, sugar and cinnamon. Cut the orange in half and push the cloves into the outside peel of the orange halves. Place oranges with cloves in the saucepan. Heat slowly over low heat for about 30 minutes or until liquid is steaming, being careful not to boil. Heat glasses in warm water before ladling mixture into glasses. Serve warm.

WHITE PEACH SANGRIA
Makes 6 servings

1 (750 ml.) bottle dry
  white wine
¾ C. peach flavored vodka
6 T. frozen lemonade
  concentrate, thawed
¼ C. sugar

1 lb. white peaches,
  pitted and sliced
¾ C. halved seedless
  red grapes
¾ C. halved seedless
  green grapes

In a large pitcher, combine white wine, peach vodka, lemonade concentrate and sugar. Mix well, until sugar is completely dissolved. Add sliced peaches, red grape halves and green grape halves. Chill mixture in refrigerator for 2 hours or overnight. To serve, pour sangria over ice into tall glasses. Ladle some peach slices and grapes into each serving.

"*In wine there is wisdom. In beer there is strength. In water there is bacteria.*"

Old German Proverb

CHAMPAGNE

Champagne refers to France's northernmost wine district where sparkling wines are made. The makers of Champagne, producers known as Champenois, are fiercely protective of the wine that made their region famous and have fought to make sure the name is used correctly. Therefore, almost any bottles labeled Champagne originate from this cold, northern French region. Most sparkling wines produced elsewhere will be labeled only as Sparkling Wine.

Champagne is made from any combination of three main wines: Pinot Noir, Pinot Meunier and Chardonnay. The grapes of the first two are black, while Chardonnay is made from white grapes. Since most champagne is white, the wine is typically made by gently pressing the juice from the grapes and quickly removing the skins before any color is imparted. Once the wine is ready, the winemaker creates his specific blend and adds bubbles by fermenting yeast and sugar in the bottle and sealing very tightly. This creates a gas that cannot escape, therefore causing the carbon dioxide to dissolve in the wine.

TIPS FOR SERVING CHAMPAGNE

Champagne is the primary wine used to celebrate holidays and special occasions. Use these simple tips to ensure your next toast of bubbly will leave a good taste in the mouths of all your guests!

- Make sure the Champagne is well chilled – at least 4 hours in the refrigerator.
- Remove the outer foil wrap. Carefully untwist, but do not remove, the wire cage.
- Use a kitchen towel or cloth napkin to cover the wire cage and cork.
- Hold the bottle at a 45° angle and point the bottle away from anyone.
- Hold the towel over the cage and cork firmly with one hand and use the other hand to twist the base of the bottle.
- After a slight pop, remove the towel and pour the Champagne into tall glasses. Use tall narrow glasses, which help the bubbles in the Champagne last longer.

EASY MARINARA SAUCE

Makes 4 cups

2 (14½ oz.) cans stewed
tomatoes
1 (6 oz.) can tomato paste
4 T. fresh chopped parsley
1 clove garlic, minced
1 tsp. dried oregano

1 tsp. salt
¼ tsp. pepper
6 T. olive oil
⅓ C. finely diced onion
½ C. white wine

In a blender or food processor, combine stewed tomatoes, tomato paste, parsley, minced garlic, dried oregano, salt and pepper. Process on high speed until smooth. In a large skillet over medium heat, heat olive oil. Add diced onion and sauté for 2 minutes. Add blended tomato mixture and white wine to skillet and let mixture simmer for 30 minutes, stirring occasionally. Use in recipes calling for marinara sauce and store in an airtight container in refrigerator or freezer.

WHITE WINE SAUCE

Makes 8 servings

1 C. heavy whipping cream   1 tsp. salt
¾ C. white wine   1 tsp. dried parsley flakes
2 T. flour

In a medium saucepan over medium high heat, combine heavy cream, white wine, flour, salt and parsley. Mix well and bring mixture to a boil. Reduce heat to low and let mixture simmer until thickened. Use as sauce for pasta or over chicken.

> **"** *Sparkling and bright in the liquid light does the wine our goblets gleam in; with hue as red as the rosy bed which a bee would choose to dream in.* **"**
>
> **Charles Fenno Hoffman**

RED WINE JELLY
Makes 5 (½ pint) jars

3½ C. red wine
½ C. fresh lemon juice

1 (2 oz.) pkg. dry pectin
4½ C. sugar

In a large saucepan over medium high heat, combine red wine, lemon juice and dry pectin. Bring mixture to a boil, stirring frequently. Mix in sugar, stirring constantly, until completely dissolved. Return mixture to a boil for 1 minute, stirring constantly. Remove from heat and, if necessary, skim foam off top of hot mixture. Ladle hot jelly into ½ pint jars that have been heated and sterilized. Pour jelly mixture to within ½″ of the top of each jar. Close each jar tightly with a 2-piece lid. Place filled, closed jars in a pan of boiling water for 5 minutes.

CHEESE PUFF APPETIZER

Makes 16 servings

2 eggs
⅔ C. flour
½ C. white wine
⅔ C. milk
½ tsp. salt

1 green onion, chopped
¾ C. shredded Swiss cheese
1 T. butter, melted
2 T. grated Parmesan
    cheese

Preheat oven to 425°. Lightly grease a 9˝ pie plate. In a medium mixing bowl, beat eggs at low speed. Mix in flour, wine, milk, salt, chopped onion, shredded Swiss cheese and melted butter by hand. Mix until well combined and pour mixture into prepared pie plate. Sprinkle grated Parmesan cheese over top and bake in oven for 30 to 35 minutes, or until puffed and golden brown. Remove from oven and let cool before cutting into small slices.

PISTACHIO WHITE WINE CHEESE BALL

Makes 16 servings

1 (8 oz.) pkg. cream cheese, softened

2 oz. crumbled Gorgonzola cheese

¼ C. shredded sharp Cheddar cheese

2 T. white wine

2 T. paprika

½ C. chopped pistachio nuts

In a medium bowl, combine cream cheese, crumbled Gorgonzola cheese, shredded sharp Cheddar cheese and white wine. Mix until well combined and form mixture into a ball. Spread paprika and chopped pistachio nuts in an even layer over a piece of waxed paper. Roll the cheese ball over the pistachio mixture until completely coated. Wrap cheese ball in waxed paper and chill in refrigerator for 6 hours before serving. Serve with various crackers.

COOKING WITH WINE

Many people have discovered the reasons behind cooking with wine. The wine intensifies and enhances delicious dishes, releasing flavors from foods that would not otherwise be noted. Most experts advise cooking with actual wines instead of liquids called "Cooking Wine" or wine flavored vinegar. Cooking wines are typically salty and can contain additives that may adversely affect the taste of the food. Also, it is preferable to use a good quality wine in the dish, though quality does not always equal expensive price tag. Look for a good quality wine that is well balanced, young and powerful, which will allow the wine to stand up to higher temperatures and longer cooking times. However, look for a wine that you would drink. Typically, if you do not enjoy the flavor of the wine, you will not enjoy the resulting cooked dish.

SIMPLE IDEAS FOR USING WINE IN COOKING

- When a recipe calls for water, replace the water with a favorite wine.

- For an easy basting liquid for grilled, baked or broiled fish, combine a light, dry white wine with melted butter. Or, mix a favorite wine into any oil to create a basting sauce for meat or poultry.

- Create a rich brown gravy for red meat by adding 1 to 2 tablespoons of a full-bodied red wine to the gravy mixture.

- Pour leftover wine into an ice cube tray and freeze for future cooking use. Simply add 1 or 2 frozen cubes to the mixture, allowing wine cubes to melt during cooking.

- When adding wine to a cooked meal, serve the same wine (or a wine from within the same family) as a beverage with the meal to balance the flavors.

CREAMED ONIONS
Makes 8 servings

2 lbs. small white onions,
  peeled
1 (750 ml.) bottle Chardonnay
1 bay leaf

¼ tsp. dried thyme
Salt to taste
1 C. heavy whipping cream
1 tsp. butter

In a large pot over medium low heat, place peeled onions. Add enough Chardonnay to cover half of the onions. Add bay leaf, dried thyme and salt, mixing well. Reduce heat and let simmer for 25 minutes. Add heavy cream and bring mixture to a boil, reduce heat and simmer until thickened. Remove from heat and stir in butter. Before serving, remove bay leaf.

ITALIAN FISH FILLETS
Makes 4 servings

2 T. olive oil
1 onion, thinly sliced
2 cloves garlic, minced
1 (14½ oz.) can diced
  tomatoes, drained

½ C. sliced black olives
1 T. fresh chopped parsley
½ C. dry white wine
1 lb. cod or haddock fillets

In a large saucepan over medium heat, heat olive oil. Add sliced onions and minced garlic and sauté until transparent and softened. Stir in drained tomatoes, sliced black olives, fresh chopped parsley and white wine. Let mixture simmer for 5 minutes. Place fillets in simmering sauce and cook for an additional 5 minutes, or until fish turns white and is heated throughout.

GRILLED CHICKEN BROCCOLI CASSEROLE

Makes 4 to 6 servings

4 skinless, boneless chicken breast halves

1 (10¾ oz.) can cream of chicken soup

1 C. white wine

1 C. mayonnaise

2 T. curry powder

4 C. fresh chopped broccoli

2 C. shredded sharp Cheddar cheese

½ C. dry breadcrumbs

Preheat grill to high heat and lightly oil the grate. Cook chicken breast halves over grill until heated throughout. Remove chicken from grill and cut into small pieces. Preheat oven to 350°. In a medium bowl, combine cream of chicken soup, white wine, mayonnaise and curry powder. Mix well and set aside. In a lightly greased 9 x 13″ baking dish, spread chopped broccoli in an even layer. Top broccoli with ⅓ of the shredded sharp Cheddar cheese. Next, spread chicken pieces in an even layer and top with another ⅓ of the shredded cheese. Pour soup mixture over cheese and top with dry breadcrumbs. Finally, sprinkle remaining ⅓ of the shredded cheese over ingredients in baking dish. Bake in oven for 40 minutes. Remove from oven and let cool for 5 minutes before serving.

WILD MUSHROOM BAKED BEANS

Makes 6 servings

2 T. olive oil
1 (3½ oz.) pkg. shiitake
 mushrooms, sliced
1 (8 oz.) pkg. baby Portobello
 mushrooms, sliced
1 C. chopped onions
2 tsp. minced garlic
2 T. flour
1 (15 oz.) can pinto beans,
 drained and rinsed

1 (15 oz.) can Great Northern
 beans, drained and rinsed
1 (15 oz.) can red kidney beans,
 drained and rinsed
1½ C. dry white wine
¾ tsp. dried thyme
1 tsp. fresh minced
 parsley

Preheat oven to 350°. In a large skillet over medium heat, place olive oil. When oil is hot, add sliced shiitake mushrooms, sliced Portobello mushrooms, chopped onions and minced garlic. Sauté mixture for 8 to 10 minutes, until softened. Stir in flour and heat for an additional 1 to 2 minutes. In a large baking dish, combine sautéed mixture, rinsed pinto beans, Great Northern beans, kidney beans, white wine and dried thyme. Mix until well combined. Bake, uncovered, in oven for 45 minutes. Before serving, sprinkle with minced parsley.

GARLIC ROASTED SHRIMP SKEWERS

Makes 4 servings

1 (.7 oz.) env. Good Seasons roasted garlic salad dressing mix

¼ C. vegetable oil

¼ C. white wine vinegar

3 T. dry white wine

1 lb. large shrimp, peeled and de-veined

1 (8 oz.) pkg. whole mushrooms

1 medium onion, cut into wedges

Soak 4 (10˝) wooden skewers in water for 30 minutes. In a medium bowl, combine salad dressing mix, vegetable oil, white wine vinegar and dry white wine. Mix until well blended and set aside ¼ cup of the mixture. Slide shrimp, whole mushrooms and onion wedges onto skewers and place kabobs in a single layer in a shallow baking dish. Pour remaining marinade over kabobs. Cover shallow dish and chill in refrigerator for 30 minutes to 1 hour. Preheat grill to medium high heat and lightly oil the grate. Drain dish, discarding the marinade. Cook kabobs on preheated grill for 3 to 4 minutes on each side, or until shrimp turn pink. During grilling, baste shrimp with reserved marinade mixture.

ARUGULA GARLIC RISOTTO

Makes 4 servings

3½ C. chicken broth
1 T. olive oil
3 cloves garlic, thinly sliced
1½ C. Arborio rice,
   uncooked

½ C. chopped onions
½ C. dry white wine
¼ tsp. salt
¼ tsp. pepper
4 C. trimmed arugula

In a small saucepan over low heat, bring chicken broth to a simmer, being careful not to boil. In a large saucepan over medium heat, place olive oil. Add sliced garlic and sauté for 3 minutes, or until garlic is lightly browned. Using a slotted spoon, remove garlic from saucepan and set aside. Add rice and chopped onions to saucepan and cook for 5 minutes. Stir in white wine, salt and pepper. Heat, stirring constantly, until wine is nearly all absorbed, about 1 minute. Add warmed chicken broth, ½ cup at a time, stirring constantly. Cook until chicken broth is absorbed before adding next batch, about 20 minutes. Remove from heat and stir in sautéed garlic and arugula. Serve immediately.

ALCOHOL CONSUMPTION

When cooking with wine, the actual amount of alcohol consumed varies, depending on the way in which the wine is used and the length of time it is heated or cooked. The following chart, from the Agricultural Research Services of the USDA, shows the amount of alcohol remaining in the dish in various cooking situations.

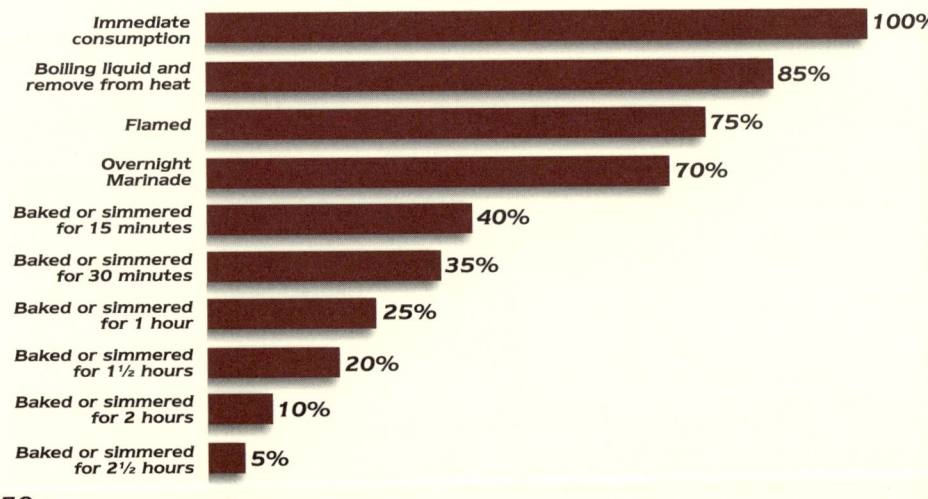

Situation	Alcohol Remaining
Immediate consumption	100%
Boiling liquid and remove from heat	85%
Flamed	75%
Overnight Marinade	70%
Baked or simmered for 15 minutes	40%
Baked or simmered for 30 minutes	35%
Baked or simmered for 1 hour	25%
Baked or simmered for 1½ hours	20%
Baked or simmered for 2 hours	10%
Baked or simmered for 2½ hours	5%

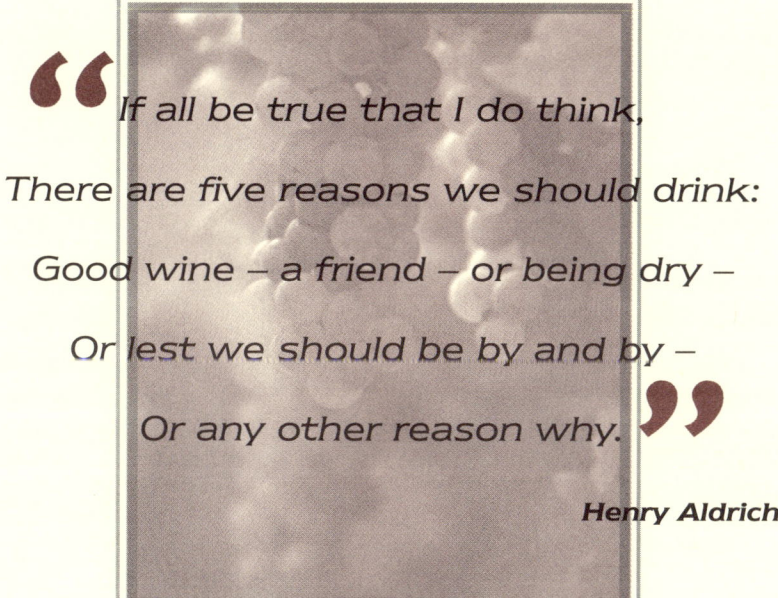

" *If all be true that I do think,*

There are five reasons we should drink:

Good wine – a friend – or being dry –

Or lest we should be by and by –

Or any other reason why. **"**

Henry Aldrich

CHAMPAGNE ROASTED TURKEY
Makes 12 servings

1 (7 lb.) whole turkey
1 ½ C. halved red seedless grapes, divided
½ tsp. salt
½ tsp. pepper
1 (750 ml.) bottle champagne
1 (14 oz.) can chicken broth
2 T. cornstarch

Preheat oven to 350°. Line a roasting pan with aluminum foil and coat aluminum foil with non-stick cooking spray. Spoon 1 cup halved grapes into the inside cavity of the turkey and season inside and outside of turkey with salt and pepper. Place turkey in roasting pan and pour champagne around the turkey in the pan. Place pan with turkey in oven and roast for 2¼ to 2½ hours, or until the turkey juice runs clear. Baste turkey with juices every 30 minutes. If turkey is browning too quickly, cover loosely with aluminum foil. In a medium saucepan over medium heat, combine chicken broth, cornstarch and some of the drippings from the roasting pan. Bring mixture to a boil, stirring constantly, until thickened. Stir in remaining ½ cup halved grapes and cook for an additional 1 to 2 minutes, or until mixture is heated throughout. Before serving, carve turkey as desired and serve with grape champagne sauce on the side.

SHRIMP & BASIL STUFFED EGGPLANT

Makes 2 servings

1 eggplant, halved
   lengthwise
½ C. olive oil, divided
Salt and pepper to taste
8 medium shrimp, peeled,
   de-veined and chopped
2 T. fresh chopped basil

2 cloves garlic, crushed
½ C. white wine
1 C. seasoned bread-
   crumbs
½ C. grated Parmesan
   cheese, divided

Preheat oven to 350°. Scoop flesh from eggplant halves and chop into pieces. Coat eggplant shells with ¼ cup olive oil and season with salt and pepper. In a large skillet over medium high heat, place remaining ¼ cup olive oil. Add chopped shrimp, basil and garlic. Sauté until shrimp turns pink, about 1 minute. Stir in chopped eggplant and season with salt and pepper. Add white wine and heat, stirring occasionally, for about 5 minutes. Transfer mixture to a large bowl and mix in breadcrumbs and ¼ cup Parmesan cheese. If mixture is too dry, stir in a little olive oil. Divide mixture evenly into eggplant shells and sprinkle remaining Parmesan cheese over top. Place eggplant shells in a baking dish and bake in oven for 30 to 40 minutes, or until eggplant is tender.

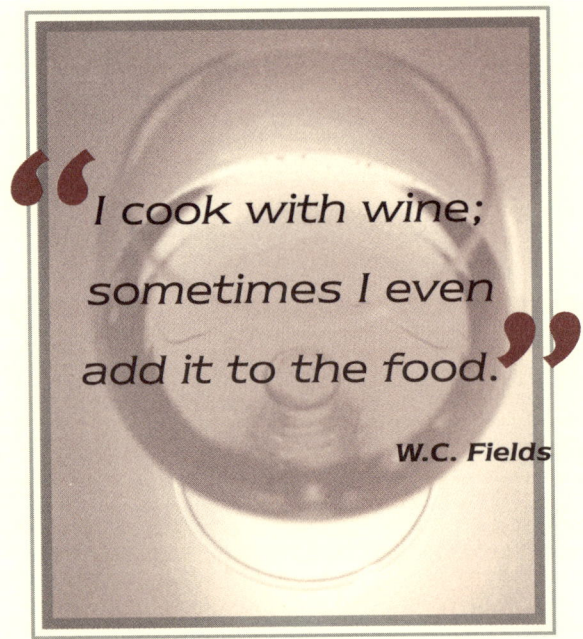

I cook with wine; sometimes I even add it to the food.

W.C. Fields

CHERRY GLAZED HAM
Makes 8 to 12 servings

6 T. Dijon mustard, divided
1 (2½ to 3½ lb.) boneless
  ham, fully cooked
1 (16½ oz.) can pitted dark
  sweet cherries

½ C. red wine
¼ C. dark brown sugar
4 tsp. cornstarch
1 T. frozen orange juice
  concentrate

Using a pastry brush, brush 4 tablespoons Dijon mustard over cooked ham and bake ham according to label directions. Meanwhile, drain cherries, reserving the syrup. In a medium saucepan over medium heat, combine reserved cherry syrup, red wine, brown sugar, cornstarch, orange juice concentrate and remaining 2 tablespoons Dijon mustard. Heat, stirring constantly, until mixture thickens and begins to boil. Set aside ⅓ cup of the sauce. Add cherries to remaining sauce and keep warm. During last 30 minutes of baking time for the ham, brush reserved sauce over ham. When ham is done, remove from oven and cut into slices. Serve with cherry sauce.

CAESAR BROILED SALMON

Makes 4 servings

¼ C. fresh lemon juice
¼ C. olive oil
3 T. dry white wine

1 (.6 oz.) env. Caesar
salad dressing mix
4 salmon steaks

In a medium bowl, combine lemon juice, olive oil, white wine and Caesar salad dressing mix. Stir until well blended and set aside ¼ cup of the mixture. Place salmon steaks in a shallow baking dish and pour remaining mixture over salmon. Place in refrigerator for 30 to 60 minutes. Remove, drain and discard marinade. Preheat broiler. On the greased rack of a broiler pan, place marinated salmon steaks. Place steaks 2″ to 4″ under broiler for 6 minutes on each side. Salmon is done when it flakes easily with a fork. Brush reserved sauce mixture over salmon and serve.

"The wine-cup is the little silver well, Where truth, if truth there be, doth dwell."

William Shakespeare

CHICKEN IN RED WINE SAUCE
Makes 12 servings

1 T. olive oil	1 T. paprika
1 T. minced garlic	1 C. brown sugar
3 lbs. skinless, boneless chicken breast halves	1 C. red wine
	Salt and pepper to taste

In a large skillet over medium high heat, heat olive oil. Add minced garlic and sauté until garlic is tender. Place chicken breast halves over garlic in skillet and cook chicken for about 10 minutes on both sides, until chicken is no longer pink in the center. Drain oil from skillet and sprinkle paprika and brown sugar over chicken. Add red wine to skillet, cover and let simmer for 15 to 20 minutes, basting chicken occasionally with cooking juices. Season with salt and pepper to taste. To serve, remove cooked chicken breast halves to a plate and carefully pour some of the red wine sauce over chicken.

SPINACH AND SAUTÉED PORTOBELLOS

Makes 4 servings

3 T. butter
2 large Portobello
   mushrooms, sliced
1 (10 oz.) pkg. frozen
   chopped spinach,
   thawed and drained
¼ tsp. dried basil

¼ tsp. salt
¼ tsp. pepper
1 clove garlic, minced
2 T. dry red wine
¼ C. grated Parmesan
   cheese

In a large skillet over medium heat, melt butter. Add sliced Portobello mushrooms, drained spinach, dried basil, salt, pepper and minced garlic. Heat, stirring occasionally, until mushrooms are tender and spinach is heated throughout. Add red wine and reduce heat to low. Bring mixture to a simmer for 1 minute. Stir in grated Parmesan cheese and serve immediately.

"When men drink, then they are rich and successful and win lawsuits and are happy and help their friends. Quickly, bring me a beaker of wine, so that I may wet my mind and say something clever."

Aristophanes

SCALLOPS IN WINE SAUCE

Makes 4 to 6 servings

1½ lbs. sea scallops
½ lb. fresh sliced
  mushrooms
1 (10¾ oz.) can cream
  of celery soup

½ C. heavy whipping cream
¼ C. dry white wine
½ tsp. salt
¼ tsp. pepper
2 T. Italian bread crumbs

Preheat oven to 450°. In an 8″ square baking dish, combine sea scallops and sliced mushrooms. In a medium bowl, combine cream of celery soup, heavy cream, white wine, salt and pepper, stirring until well mixed. Pour mixture over scallops and mushrooms and sprinkle top with bread crumbs. Bake in oven for 25 to 30 minutes, or until casserole is bubbling and scallops are cooked throughout.

WINE SMOTHERED STEAK & PEPPERS

Makes 6 to 8 servings

2 T. vegetable oil
½ lb. fresh sliced mushrooms
1 red bell pepper, thinly sliced
1 green bell pepper, thinly sliced
2 lbs. beef round steak, cut into thin strips

2 onions, sliced
1 tsp. salt
1 tsp. pepper
1 (10¾ oz.) can cream of mushroom soup
¾ C. dry red wine
⅔ C. water
1½ tsp. soy sauce

In a large skillet over medium high heat, heat oil. Add sliced mushrooms, sliced red bell pepper, sliced green bell pepper and sliced onions. Sauté vegetables for 4 to 5 minutes, or until tender and remove vegetables to a bowl. Reserve drippings in skillet. Season steak strips with salt and pepper and add to drippings in skillet. In a medium bowl, combine cream of mushroom soup, red wine and water. Mix well and pour mixture over steak in skillet. Reduce heat to low, cover and let simmer for 45 minutes. Add sautéed vegetables and soy sauce and continue to heat for 8 to 10 minutes, until sauce is thickened.

SIMPLE GOLDEN CASSEROLE

Makes 6 servings

2 small onions, chopped
1 tsp. garlic powder
2 C. cooked, cubed ham
1 lb. pork sausage,
    cooked and drained
2 C. canned navy beans,
    drained

2 tsp. dried parsley
⅓ C. white wine
¼ tsp. ground cloves
Salt and pepper to taste

Preheat oven to 300°. In a large skillet over medium heat, combine chopped onions and garlic powder. Sauté for 2 to 3 minutes, until onions are tender. Add cooked ham, cooked pork sausage, drained navy beans, dried parsley, white wine and ground cloves. Season with salt and pepper to taste and mix well. Transfer mixture to a 9 x 13″ baking dish. Bake, uncovered, in oven for 30 minutes.

FRENCH ONION SOUP

Makes 4 to 6 servings

3 T. butter
3 large onions, thinly sliced
3 (14 oz.) cans beef broth
1 C. apple cider
½ tsp. pepper
½ C. grated Parmesan
cheese

⅓ C. dry red wine
4 to 6 (1″ thick) slices French
bread, toasted
½ C. shredded Swiss
cheese

In a large soup pot over medium heat, melt butter. Add sliced onions and sauté for 25 minutes, stirring occasionally, until onions are golden. Add beef broth, apple cider and pepper and bring mixture to a boil. Reduce heat to low and stir in Parmesan cheese and red wine, until cheese is melted and soup is heated throughout, about 3 to 5 minutes. Preheat broiler. Place lightly toasted French bread slices on a baking sheet and sprinkle an even amount of shredded Swiss cheese over slices. Place under broiler for 3 to 5 minutes, or until cheese is melted. To serve, ladle soup into bowls and top each serving with a slice of toasted bread. Serve immediately.

"*No longer are her invitations sought and fought for eagerly, her parties once so popular are now attended meagerly; a blunder unforgivable made life no longer livable, for she served the sparkling burgundy in glasses made for port.*"

Newman Levy

WINE STEMWARE

You've probably seen wine served in glasses of several different shapes and sizes. The reasoning behind all the different stemware is that it is widely believed that the glass a certain wine is served in can detract from or enhance the enjoyment of the beverage. Here are some of the basic rules for serving wine.

SPARKLING WINE

Champagne and sparkling wine should be served in tall, tapered flutes, which are designed to keep the bubbles in the wine active. The tall sides of the glass keep too much air from entering the glass that would make the wine go flat.

WHITE WINE

White wine should be served in glasses that hold 8 to 14 ounces. The rounded part of the glass should be about medium in size and taper inward at the top. When serving, only fill the glass to about ⅓ of its capacity. Hold the glass by the stem, as the heat from your hand will quickly warm the wine.

RED WINE

Red wine should be served in glasses that hold 10 to 16 ounces with a slightly larger, rounder bowl than a white wine glass. The glass should taper inward slightly at the top, which helps hold the aroma of the wine in the glass. Hold the glass by the stem, as the heat from your hand will affect red wines. The only exception to this rule is when drinking Cognac or brandy, with which warming is desirable.

THICKNESS

It is preferable to serve wine in glasses made of thin glass. Heavier, thicker glasses have more influence over the temperature of the wine.

CLEANLINESS

Soap or a film left from dish detergent will negatively affect the taste and smell of the wine. At home, thoroughly rinse wine glasses in plain hot water instead of using soap. Rinse several times and, if possible, use filtered water.

RED WINE SPAGHETTI SAUCE

Makes 2 to 4 cups

1 lb. ground Italian sausage
2 large onions, chopped
6 cloves garlic, crushed
2 C. red wine
1 (8 oz.) can beef broth
2 (29 oz.) cans pureed
   tomatoes
3 to 5 fresh tomatoes,
   chopped

2 bay leaves
¼ tsp. dried thyme
1 tsp. dried oregano
½ tsp. dried basil
2 T. crushed red peppers
Salt and pepper to taste

In a large saucepan over medium heat, cook ground sausage until heated throughout. Drain off fat and add chopped onions to cooked sausage in saucepan. Continue to sauté until onions are golden brown, about 5 to 10 minutes. Add crushed garlic and heat for an additional 1 to 2 minutes. Add red wine and bring mixture to a boil. In a large deep pot over medium high heat, bring beef broth to a boil. Add sausage and onion mixture and continue to boil until liquid is almost completely evaporated. Add pureed tomatoes and fresh chopped tomatoes. Mix well and stir in bay leaves, dried thyme, dried oregano, dried basil and crushed red peppers. Return mixture to a boil, reduce heat and let simmer for 30 minutes, stirring frequently. When sauce has reduced to desired consistency, remove bay leaves and season with salt and pepper to taste.

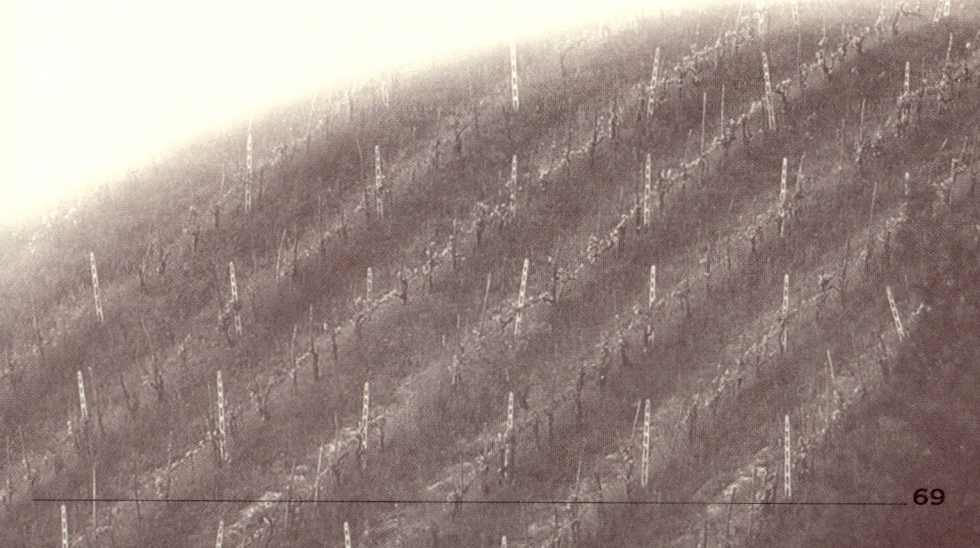

SHRIMP LASAGNA

Makes 6 servings

1 (16 oz.) pkg. lasagna
  noodles
2 T. butter
1 onion, chopped
1 (12 oz.) container cottage
  cheese
1 (8 oz.) pkg. cream cheese
2 tsp. dried basil
½ tsp. salt
1/8 tsp. pepper
1 egg
2 (10 ¾ oz.) can cream
  of mushroom soup

⅓ C. milk
1 clove garlic, minced
½ C. white wine
½ lb. scallops
½ lb. flounder fillets
½ lb. shrimp, peeled
  and de-veined
¼ C. shredded
  mozzarella cheese
2 T. grated Parmesan
  cheese

In a large pot of lightly salted water, cook lasagna noodles until al dente. Drain pot of water and set aside. In a medium skillet over medium high heat, melt butter. Add chopped onion and sauté until softened and transparent. Remove from heat and stir in cottage cheese, cream cheese, dried basil, salt, pepper and egg. Mix well and set aside. In a separate bowl, combine cream of mushroom soup, milk, minced garlic, white wine, scallops, flounder fillets and shrimp. Toss until evenly coated and set aside. Preheat oven to 350°. To assemble lasagna, in a greased 9 x 13″ baking dish place a thin layer of the shrimp mixture and top with $1/5$ of the cooked noodles and half of the cheese mixture. Top with another $1/5$ of the noodles, half of the remaining seafood mixture, another $1/5$ noodles and the remaining cheese mixture. Finally, top with another $1/5$ noodles, remaining seafood mixture and remaining noodles. Sprinkle shredded mozzarella cheese and grated Parmesan cheese over top. Bake in oven for 45 to 60 minutes, remove from oven and let stand for 10 minutes before serving.

"*Burgundy was the winiest wine, the central, essential and typical wine, the soul and greatest common measure of all the kindly wines of the earth.*"

Charles Edward Montague

BEEF BURGUNDY SOUP

Makes 5 to 6 servings

1 T. vegetable oil
1½ lbs. beef, cut into
    1″ pieces
1 tsp. dried thyme
½ tsp. salt
½ tsp. pepper
1 (14 oz.) can beef broth
½ C. Burgundy or other
    red wine

3 cloves garlic, minced
2 C. baby carrots
1 C. frozen whole pearl
    onions
3 T. cornstarch
2 T. water
1 (8 oz.) pkg. frozen
    sugar snap peas

In a large soup pot over medium high heat, heat vegetable oil.
Add beef in batches and brown until cooked throughout. Drain off
fat, keeping browned beef in the pot. Season with dried thyme,
salt and pepper. Add beef broth, wine and minced garlic. Bring
mixture to a boil, reduce heat to low, cover and let simmer for 1
hour. Stir in baby carrots and whole pearl onions, cover and let
simmer for 30 to 45 minutes, stirring occasionally. Soup is ready
when beef and vegetables are tender. In a small bowl, combine
cornstarch and water, stirring until cornstarch is completely dissolved. Add cornstarch mixture to beef mixture and stir for 1 minute, until soup is thickened. Stir in sugar snap peas and continue
to heat for 3 to 4 minutes. To serve, ladle soup into bowls.

CHICKEN
A LA CRÈME FRAICHE

Makes 4 to 6 servings

1 to 2 T. vegetable oil
6 skinless, boneless chicken
   breast halves
¼ C. white wine
Salt and pepper to taste
1 (8 oz.) pkg. pasta, any kind
1 large onion, chopped

1 T. minced garlic
2 (8 oz.) pkgs. fresh
   sliced mushrooms
2 C. crème fraiche
3 T. sour cream
½ C. grated
   Parmesan cheese

In a large skillet over medium high heat, place vegetable oil. Add chicken breast halves and sauté until chicken is lightly browned. Add white wine and salt and pepper to taste. Reduce heat and let simmer for 15 to 20 minutes, or until chicken is cooked throughout. Meanwhile, in a large pot of lightly salted boiling water, cook pasta until al dente. Drain pot and set aside. When chicken is cooked throughout, remove chicken from skillet and cut into small pieces and set aside. Add chopped onions and minced garlic to same skillet over medium heat and sauté until tender. Add mushrooms and continue to heat until softened. Return cubed chicken to skillet and add crème fraiche and sour cream. Mix well and continue to cook until mixture is heated throughout. Divide cooked pasta evenly among dinner plates and place chicken mixture over pasta on each plate. Sprinkle grated Parmesan cheese over each serving.

WINE COUNTRY BEEF STROGANOFF

Makes 4 servings

1 (12 oz.) pkg. wide
  egg noodles
1 lb. beef sirloin
3 T. olive oil, divided
¾ C. finely chopped onions
1½ tsp. minced garlic
¾ lb. fresh shiitake
  mushrooms, thinly sliced
¾ C. Pinot Noir or any
  dry red wine

3 T. Cognac
2 T. prepared oyster sauce
1½ C. heavy whipping
  cream
1½ tsp. cornstarch
6 T. sour cream
Salt and pepper to taste
2 T. fresh chopped
  parsley, optional

In a large saucepan or pot over high heat, bring 12 to 16 cups water to a boil. Add egg noodles and return to a boil, stirring occasionally, until noodles are barely tender. Drain pot and transfer pasta to a serving bowl. If necessary, de-bone beef sirloin and trim any fat. Rinse and pat dry the beef sirloin. Cut sirloin, against the grain, into ⅛″ thick slices. In a large saucepan or 14″ wok over medium high heat, add 1 tablespoon olive oil. When oil is hot, add beef slices and cook about 2 to 3 minutes, until beef is browned on the edges but still slightly pink in the center. Transfer beef to a plate and keep warm. Add remaining 2 tablespoons olive oil to wok. Place chopped onions and minced garlic in wok and sauté until softened, about 3 to 5 minutes. Add sliced mushrooms and stir until mushrooms begin to brown. Mix in Pinot Noir, Cognac and prepared oyster sauce. Mix lightly and bring to a boil. Reduce heat and let simmer for about 5 minutes. Add heavy cream and continue to simmer. In a small bowl, combine cornstarch and 1 tablespoon cold water. Mix until a smooth paste forms and add to mushroom mixture. Bring mixture to a boil for 2 minutes, until thickened. Add sour cream and cooked beef slices and stir until heated throughout. Add salt and pepper to taste. To serve, place egg noodles on serving plates and top with the beef and sauce mixture. If desired, garnish with chopped parsley.

CHICKEN N' ANGEL HAIR PASTA

Makes 6 servings

¼ C. butter
1 (¾ oz.) pkg. Italian
   salad dressing mix
½ C. white wine
1 (10¾ oz.) can cream
   of mushroom soup

1 (4 oz.) pkg. cream
   cheese with chives
6 skinless, boneless
   chicken breast halves
1 lb. angle hair pasta

Preheat oven to 325°. In a large saucepan over low heat, melt butter. Stir in Italian dressing mix, white wine and cream of mushroom soup. Add cream cheese and stir until mixture is melted and smooth. Cook until mixture is heated throughout, being careful not to boil. In a 9 x 13″ baking dish, place chicken breast halves in a single layer. Pour sauce mixture over chicken breast halves and bake in oven for 1 hour. Meanwhile, in a large pot of lightly salted water, cook angel hair pasta until al dente. Drain pasta and arrange on plates. Set one chicken breast half over pasta on each plate and drizzle with sauce.

Wine is one of the most civilized things in the world and one of the most natural things in the world that has been brought to the greatest perfection, and it offers a greater range for enjoyment and appreciation than, possibly, any other purely sensory thing.

Ernest Hemingway

MOZZARELLA CHICKEN IN WHITE WINE

Makes 4 servings

4 skinless, boneless
  chicken breast
½ C. butter, divided
Salt and pepper to taste
4 slices mozzarella cheese

1 egg, beaten
2 C. flour
1 C. seasoned breadcrumbs
2 tsp. minced garlic
1 C. dry white wine

Preheat oven to 350°. Place chicken breasts between two sheets of waxed paper and, using a meat mallet, pound meat to ¼″ thickness. Spread ¼ cup of the butter over one side of each chicken breast and season with salt and pepper. Place 1 slice of mozzarella cheese over buttered side of each chicken breast. Roll up chicken breasts so cheese is on the inside and secure with toothpicks. Place flour on a plate and place beaten egg in a shallow bowl. Spread out bread crumbs on a separate plate. Dip rolled chicken breasts in flour first, then into the egg and then into the breadcrumbs. In a 9 x 13″ baking dish, place coated chicken breasts. To make sauce, in a medium saucepan over medium heat, place remaining ¼ cup butter. Heat until butter is melted and add minced garlic and white wine. Let mixture simmer, stirring occasionally, for 5 minutes. Pour simmering sauce mixture over chicken in baking dish. Bake in oven for 30 to 45 minutes.

" A man cannot make him

laugh- but that is no marvel;

he drinks no wine. "

William Shakespeare

ROSEMARY GARLIC SHRIMP
Makes 4 servings

- 1 lb. medium-size fresh shrimp, unpeeled
- 2 T. butter or margarine
- ¼ C. olive oil
- 1 head garlic
- ½ C. dry white wine
- 2 T. white wine vinegar
- 1 T. lemon juice
- 3 dried red chile peppers
- 3 bay leaves
- 1 tsp. salt
- 2 T. fresh chopped rosemary
- 1 tsp. dried oregano
- ½ tsp. crushed red peppers

Peel the shrimp, leaving the tail on. If desired, de-vein shrimp and set aside. In a large skillet over medium high heat, place butter and olive oil. Cut garlic head in half crosswise and separate and peel the individual cloves. Add garlic cloves to butter mixture and sauté for 2 minutes. Add white wine, vinegar, lemon juice, dried red chile peppers, bay leaves, salt, chopped rosemary, dried oregano and crushed red peppers. Continue to cook for 1 minute, stirring constantly, until thoroughly heated. Add prepared shrimp and cook for an additional 5 to 6 minutes, or until shrimp turns pink. If desired, serve over cooked pasta.

HAVARTI BAKED CHICKEN

Makes 4 servings

4 skinless, boneless
   chicken breast halves
Italian dressing
1 T. butter
1 T. white wine
1 T. Worcestershire sauce
½ tsp. garlic salt

1 (8 oz.) pkg. fresh sliced
   mushrooms
Salt to taste
2 (4 oz.) cans whole
   green chili peppers, drained
4 oz. Havarti cheese
   with dill, sliced

In a baking dish, place chicken breast halves. Pour Italian dressing over chicken and marinate in refrigerator for 30 minutes to 1 hour. Preheat oven to 400°. Place chicken in a 9 x 13″ baking dish and discard marinade. Bake in oven for 25 minutes, or until chicken is cooked throughout. Meanwhile, in a medium saucepan over medium high heat, place butter. Heat until butter is melted and bubbling. Add white wine, Worcestershire sauce and garlic salt. Bring mixture to a boil and stir in mushrooms. Reduce heat to low, cover and simmer until mushrooms are tender, about 3 to 5 minutes. Season with salt. Slice chili peppers lengthwise. Remove chicken from oven and place pepper slices and 1 slice Havarti cheese over each chicken breast. Return to oven until cheese has melted. Before serving, pour mushroom sauce mixture over chicken.

HERBED CHICKEN SOUP
Makes 10 servings

½ (2 to 3 lb.) whole chicken
2 parsnips, peeled and chopped
1 medium head garlic, peeled
2 large onions, chopped
5 carrots, chopped
2 zucchini, chopped
½ C. fresh chopped parsley
2 stalks celery, chopped
2 potatoes, peeled and chopped

1 sweet potato, peeled and cubed
1 (2 oz.) env. chicken vegetable soup mix
1 T. dried oregano
1 tsp. paprika
8 C. water
½ (750 ml.) bottle white wine
Salt and pepper to taste

Clean and thoroughly dry the chicken. In a large soup pot or Dutch oven over high heat, combine whole chicken, chopped parsnips, peeled garlic, chopped onions, chopped carrots, chopped zucchini, chopped parsley, chopped celery, chopped potatoes, cubed sweet potato, soup mix, dried oregano, paprika, water and wine. Cover and bring to a boil. Let boil for 30 minutes. Carefully remove chicken from boiling mixture and strip meat from the bones. Add chicken meat back to pot and season soup with salt and pepper to taste. Reduce heat to low and simmer for an additional 90 minutes.

CLASSIC SPAGHETTI

Makes 8 servings

1 lb. spaghetti
2 T. olive oil, divided
8 slices bacon, chopped
1 onion, chopped
1 clove garlic, minced
¼ C. dry white wine

4 eggs
½ C. plus 2 T. grated
   Parmesan cheese, divided
Salt and pepper to taste
2 T. fresh chopped parsley

In a large pot of lightly salted water, cook spaghetti until al dente. Drain pot of water and add 1 tablespoon olive oil. Toss until evenly coated and set aside. In a large skillet over medium high heat, cook chopped bacon until crisp. Remove bacon from skillet and reserve 2 tablespoons bacon drippings. Add remaining 1 tablespoon olive oil to skillet and add chopped onion. Cover skillet and cook over medium high heat until onion is transparent and softened. Add minced garlic and sauté for 1 additional minute. Return cooked bacon to skillet and add drained spaghetti. Toss until spaghetti is evenly coated, adding additional olive oil if needed. Add beaten eggs to hot mixture and toss constantly until eggs are barely set. Add ½ cup grated Parmesan cheese and toss quickly. Mix in salt and pepper to taste. To serve, place spaghetti on serving plates and garnish with additional 2 tablespoons grated Parmesan cheese and fresh chopped parsley.

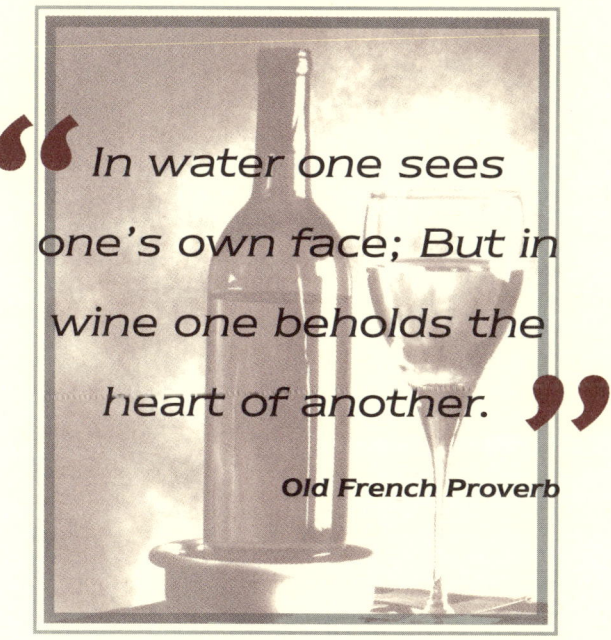

In water one sees one's own face; But in wine one beholds the heart of another.

Old French Proverb

"
This wine, petulant and clear,

Soothes our sense, and calms our fear;

When in joy we tap the cask

All our dreams bring what we ask.

Drink it! Drink it! Kindly Friend,

Then our cares will swiftly end,

Drink to you, then drink to me,

Pledge our dual prosperity.
"

Old French Poem

TIPS FOR SERVING WINE

- Instead of chilling wine in the freezer, fill a stainless steel bucket with ice water. Place the wine bottle directly in the ice water for 10 minutes.

- Place sparkling wines in the refrigerator for at least 4 hours before serving. If you are in a time crunch, place the bottle in a bucket of ice water for 20 to 30 minutes.

- Fill wine glasses slightly less than half full. This will allow for the wine to breathe.

- A safe estimate for entertaining would be to provide a half bottle of wine per guest per hour.

- To easily decant bottle-aged wine, insert an unbleached coffee filter into the neck of a glass decanter. Slowly pour the wine through the filter, removing any solids.

- Always have non-alcoholic beverages available, so the wine is not forced upon the guests.

BEEF BURGUNDY FILET MIGNON
Makes 8 serving

4 C. plus 1 tsp. Burgundy
   or other red wine, divided
1½ C. vegetable oil
1½ C. soy sauce
2 C. oyster sauce
1 T. minced garlic

1½ tsp. dried oregano
8 (6 oz.) fillets filet mignon
½ C. butter, softened
2 T. minced green onions
1 T. white pepper

In a medium saucepan over medium heat, combine 4 cups Burgundy wine, vegetable oil, soy sauce, oyster sauce, minced garlic and dried oregano. Bring mixture to a boil and remove from heat. Chill sauce mixture in refrigerator for 1 hour. In a 9 x 13″ baking dish, place filet mignon fillets. Pour chilled sauce over filet mignon and cover tightly with aluminum foil. Return to refrigerator for at least 5 hours. In a medium bowl, cream together butter and remaining 1 teaspoon Burgundy wine. Mix in minced green onions and white pepper, cover tightly and refrigerate. Preheat grill to high heat and lightly oil the grate. Preheat oven to 200°. Place marinated filet mignon on hot grill and cook to desired doneness, turning once. Remove from grill and place in a clean 9 x 13″ baking dish. Place dollops of the butter mixture over grilled fillets and bake in oven for 1 to 2 minutes, until butter is melted.

VINEYARD CHICKEN CACCIATORE

Makes 4 servings

2 C. flour
½ tsp. salt
¼ tsp. pepper
1 (4 lb.) chicken, cut into pieces
2 T. vegetable oil
1 onion, chopped
2 cloves garlic, minced
1 green bell pepper, chopped

1 (14½ oz.) can diced tomatoes
½ tsp. dried oregano
½ C. white wine
2 C. fresh mushrooms, quartered
Additional salt and pepper to taste

In a large plastic ziplock bag, combine flour, salt and pepper. Add chicken pieces and close bag. Toss until chicken is completely coated. In a large skillet over medium high heat, place vegetable oil. Add chicken pieces and fry until browned on both sides and cooked throughout. Remove cooked chicken to a plate. Add chopped onion, minced garlic, chopped green bell pepper and sauté until softened and slightly browned. Return chicken to skillet and add tomatoes, dried oregano and white wine. Reduce heat, cover skillet and let simmer for 30 minutes. Add quartered mushrooms and season with salt and pepper to taste. Let simmer for an additional 10 minutes before serving.

CHICKEN CORDON BLEU
Makes 6 servings

6 skinless, boneless
  chicken breast halves
6 slices Swiss cheese
6 thin slices cooked ham
3 T. flour
1 tsp. paprika

6 T. butter
½ C. dry white wine
1 tsp. chicken bouillon
  granules
1 T. cornstarch
1 C. heavy whipping cream

If chicken breast halves are too thick, place chicken between two sheets of waxed paper and, using a meat mallet, pound meat to desired thickness. Place one Swiss cheese slice and one thin ham slice over each chicken breast half. Fold the edges of the chicken up and over the ham and cheese and secure with toothpicks. In a shallow bowl, combine flour and paprika. Roll chicken pieces in flour mixture until coated on all sides. In a large skillet over medium high heat, place butter. When butter has melted, add chicken and heat until chicken is browned on all sides. Add white wine and chicken bouillon granules.

Mix lightly, reduce heat and cover. Let simmer for 30 minutes, until chicken is cooked throughout. Remove toothpicks and transfer chicken pieces to a serving platter. In a small bowl, combine cornstarch and heavy cream. Using a wire whisk, blend cream mixture slowly and add to liquid in skillet. Cook, stirring frequently, until sauce is thickened. Pour mixture over chicken on serving platter. Serve warm.

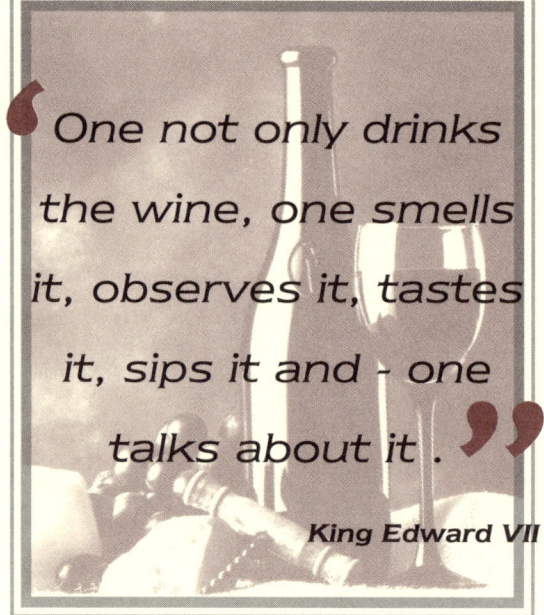

" One not only drinks the wine, one smells it, observes it, tastes it, sips it and - one talks about it . "

King Edward VII

HALIBUT CASSEROLE
Makes 4 servings

5 T. butter or margarine, divided
1 medium onion, thinly sliced
½ C. dry white wine
2 lbs. halibut fillets
Milk
3 T. flour

1½ tsp. salt
⅛ tsp. pepper
1 (8½ oz.) can small peas, drained
1½ C. Chinese noodles

In a medium saucepan over medium heat, place 2 tablespoons butter. Add sliced onion and sauté until softened. Add white wine and mix well. Cut halibut fillets into 2″ pieces and add to saucepan. Continue to heat until fish flakes easily with a fork. Drain juices from saucepan into a large measuring cup. Add enough milk to juices to make 2 cups. Set aside liquid and cooked fish. Add remaining 3 tablespoons butter to same skillet and place over medium high heat. When butter is melted, stir in flour, salt and pepper. Gradually stir in liquid mixture and heat, stirring constantly, until mixture is thickened and smooth. Add drained peas and cooked fish pieces to sauce mixture. Continue to cook until casserole is heated throughout. Before serving, sprinkle Chinese noodles over fish.

VERMOUTH POT ROAST
Makes 12 servings

3½ lbs. rump roast
½ C. flour
Pepper to taste
¼ C. butter

½ (1 oz.) env. dry onion
  soup mix
1 (10¾ oz.) can cream
  of mushroom soup
½ C. dry vermouth*

Preheat oven to 325°. Cut rump roast into pieces. In a large bowl, combine flour and pepper. Mix lightly and add rump roast pieces. Coat rump roast in flour mixture and remove from bowl, shaking off excess. In a large pot over medium high heat, place butter. When butter is melted, add coated roast pieces and cook, until browned on all sides. Transfer roast pieces to a large baking dish with a lid. In a small bowl, combine dry onion soup mix, cream of mushroom soup and dry vermouth. Mix well and pour mixture over roast. Cover baking dish and bake in oven for 3 hours, or until roast reaches desired doneness.

*Vermouth is wine that, typically, has been infused with herbs, alcohol, sugar, caramel and water.

COUNTRY STYLE PORK RIB CASSEROLE

Makes 8 servings

1 lb. country style pork ribs
Salt and pepper to taste
1 tsp. vegetable oil
¼ C. dry white wine
½ C. water
1 T. caraway seeds

1 T. brown sugar
1 lb. sauerkraut, drained
1 medium red apple,
  cored and diced
1 lb. carrots, peeled and
  coarsely chopped

Preheat oven to 350°. Season pork ribs with salt and pepper to taste. In a large deep skillet over medium high heat, place vegetable oil. Cook ribs, turning occasionally, until well browned on all sides. Add dry white wine, water, caraway seeds and brown sugar. Continue to heat, stirring frequently, until brown sugar is completely dissolved. Stir in drained sauerkraut, diced apple and chopped carrots. Mix well and transfer mixture to a large baking dish. Bake, covered, in oven for 2½ hours. Check casserole occasionally, adding water as needed, if mixture looks too dry.

> *A bottle of wine contains more philosophy than all the books in the world.*
>
> **Louis Pasteur**

SLOW COOKER CHICKEN WITH MUSHROOMS

Makes 4 servings

1 (10¾ oz.) can cream
  of mushroom soup
1 tsp. dried minced onion
1 tsp. dried parsley flakes
¼ C. white wine
¼ tsp. garlic powder
1 T. milk

1 (4 oz.) can mushroom
  pieces, drained
Salt and pepper to taste
4 boneless, skinless
  chicken breast halves
  breast halves

In the pot of a slow cooker, combine cream of mushroom soup, dried minced onion, dried parsley flakes, white wine, garlic powder, milk and drained mushroom pieces. Mix lightly and season with salt and pepper. Add chicken breast halves and cover with soup mixture. Cook at low setting for 5 to 6 hours or at the high setting for 3 to 4 hours.

THE PERFECT PAIR

Serving wine with food can be one of the great complexities in the world of fine cuisine. There are certain wines that will enhance the flavor of the food better than others. However, do not feel obliged to serve a red wine with juicy sirloin if you enjoy only white wines – the choice is yours! Also, when cooking with wine in the dish, it is always a good choice to serve that same wine with the meal. Below are the traditional combinations for pairing wine with foods.

When serving:	Try tasting:
Red meat or red meat dishes	Full-bodied, young red wine
Dishes with red sauces	Full-bodied, young, robust red wine
Soups with root vegetables or beef stock	Full-bodied, earthy red wine
Seafood, poultry, pork or veal	Dry white wine or fortified wine

Dishes with light, cream sauces	Dry white wine or fortified wine
Seafood soups or bouillabaisse	Crisp, dry white wine
Sweet desserts	Sweet white wine or sweet fortified wine
Poultry, vegetable soups or consommé	Dry, fortified wine
Regional cuisine	Regional wine

BELOW ARE SOME BASIC MENUS FOR SERVING WINE

Serve a dry or crisp white wine with Cheese Puff Appetizers (page 40) and Chicken n' Angel Hair Pasta (page 78), Rosemary Garlic Shrimp (page 82) or Halibut Casserole (page 96).

Serve a full-bodied red wine with Beef Burgundy Soup (page 73) and Wine Smothered Steak & Peppers (page 62) or Wine Country Beef Stroganoff (page 76).

ARTICHOKE VEAL CUTLETS
Makes 2 servings

¼ C. flour
¼ tsp. salt
¼ tsp. pepper
½ lb. veal cutlets
¼ C. butter

1 (14 oz.) can artichoke hearts, drained and quartered
1 T. fresh lemon juice
½ C. dry white wine

In a shallow baking dish, combine flour, salt and pepper and mix well. Add veal cutlets and coat evenly with flour mixture. In a large skillet over medium heat, place butter. When butter is melted, add coated veal cutlets and cook until browned on both sides. Add quartered artichoke hearts, lemon juice and white wine. Mix well and let cook for 2 to 3 minutes, or until mixture is heated throughout. Serve immediately.

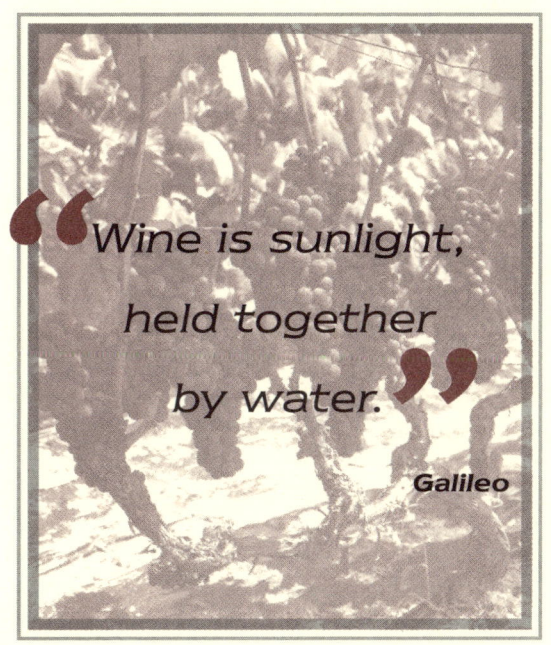

" *Wine is sunlight,*

held together

by water. "

Galileo

VANILLA WINE CAKE

Makes 1 bundt cake

1 (18¼ oz.) pkg. white
cake mix
1 (5 oz.) pkg. instant vanilla
pudding mix
1 tsp. nutmeg

¾ C. vegetable oil
¾ C. white wine
4 eggs
Powdered sugar
Fresh sliced strawberries

Preheat oven to 350°. Grease and lightly flour a 10″ bundt cake pan. In a medium mixing bowl, combine white cake mix, instant vanilla pudding mix, nutmeg, vegetable oil, white wine and eggs. Beat at medium speed for 5 minutes. Bake in oven for 50 minutes, or until a toothpick inserted in center of cake comes out clean. Remove from oven and let cake cool on a wire rack for 10 minutes before removing cake from pan. Sift powdered sugar lightly over cake and garnish with fresh sliced strawberries.

Variation: To make a textured crust, after the bundt cake pan has been greased, flour it with cocoa powder or cinnamon instead of plain white flour before adding the cake batter.

TIRAMISU
Makes 12 servings

5 egg yolks
½ C. sugar, divided
½ C. Marsala wine
1 C. heavy whipped
    cream, chilled
1 lb. mascarpone cheese

2 C. strong brewed coffee,
    room temperature
½ C. brandy
1 T. vanilla
48 ladyfinger cookies
3 T. cocoa powder

In a double boiler over medium heat, combine egg yolks and ¼ cup sugar. Using a wire whisk, beat until smooth. Mix in Marsala and continue to heat, beating frequently, until soft mounds form, about 5 to 10 minutes. Transfer mixture to a bowl, cover and refrigerate for 30 minutes. Meanwhile, in a medium mixing bowl, beat heavy cream and 2 tablespoons sugar at medium speed until soft peaks form. Fold in mascarpone cheese and chilled Marsala mixture. Cover and refrigerate for 1 hour. In a small bowl, combine coffee, remaining 2 tablespoons sugar, brandy and vanilla. In the bottom of a 9 x13″ baking dish, arrange 16 ladyfingers. Spoon about 1 tablespoon of the coffee mixture over each cookie. Spoon ⅓ of the mascarpone mixture in an even layer over cookies. Sprinkle 1 tablespoon cocoa powder over mixture and repeat layers twice more. Cover and refrigerate for 5 hours. Cut into squares and serve.

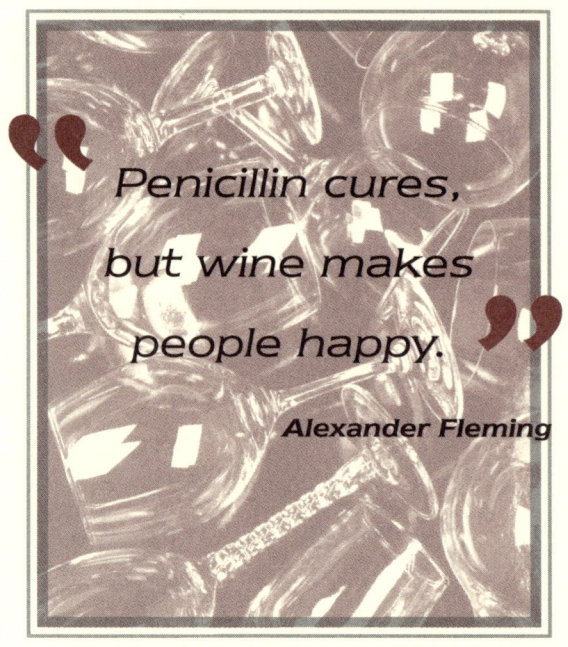

Penicillin cures, but wine makes people happy.

Alexander Fleming

SWEET ITALIAN FRIED COOKIES

Makes 6 dozen

2½ C. red wine	2½ C. vegetable oil
12 C. flour	1 qt. vegetable oil
2 C. water	1 C. honey

In a medium saucepan over medium heat, place red wine. Cook until wine is warmed, remove from heat and stir in flour. Stir in 2 cups water. Turn dough out onto a lightly floured flat surface and knead by hand. If consistency is too dry, mix in a little more water. Roll out dough into a long thin log and cut into 2″ pieces. Lay cut cookie dough on flat side and run a fork over the dough to create ridges. In a large pot over medium high heat, place vegetable oil. Heat oil until very hot and carefully lower dough into oil. Fry cookies until medium brown, turning with a slotted spoon if necessary. Remove cookies to paper towels to drain. In same medium saucepan over medium heat, place honey. When honey is warmed and turns to a very thin liquid, roll fried cookies in honey and place on a serving platter. Allow honey to cool before serving.

GLAZED BLACKBERRY WINE CAKE

Makes 1 bundt cake

1 (18 ¼ oz.) pkg.
  white cake mix
1 (3 oz.) pkg. blackberry
  gelatin
4 eggs

½ C. vegetable oil
1½ C. blackberry wine,
  divided
1½ C. powdered sugar

Preheat oven to 325°. Grease and lightly flour a 10″ bundt pan. In a large mixing bowl, combine cake mix and gelatin mix. Form a well in the center of the dry mixture and add eggs, vegetable oil and 1 cup blackberry wine. Beat at low speed until mixture is blended. Increase speed to medium and beat for 4 minutes. Pour batter evenly into prepared bundt pan. Bake in oven for 40 to 45 minutes, or until a toothpick inserted in center of cake comes out clean. Meanwhile, to prepare glaze, in a small bowl, combine powdered sugar and remaining ½ cup blackberry wine. Mix well, adding more wine or powdered sugar to reach desired consistency. Remove cake from oven and, while cake is still warm, pour half of the glaze mixture over cake. Set aside for 10 minutes before removing cake from pan. Let cake cool completely before pouring remaining glaze over top.

WALNUT WINE TREATS

Makes 42 servings

¾ C. chocolate chips

¼ C. honey

2½ C. crushed vanilla wafer cookies

⅓ C. sweet red wine

2 C. ground walnuts

Sugar

In a medium saucepan over low heat, combine chocolate chips and honey. Heat, stirring constantly, until chocolate is melted. Remove from heat and stir in crushed vanilla wafers, sweet red wine and ground walnuts. Mix until well combined and shape mixture into 1″ balls. Place sugar in a single layer on a large piece of waxed paper and roll balls in sugar until lightly coated. Place walnut wine treats on a serving platter, cover and place in refrigerator overnight.

WINE SHERBET

Makes 4 servings

2 C. white wine
Juice of 2 lemons
Juice of 1 orange
1 C. sugar

1 C. milk or heavy
  whipping cream
Fresh mint sprigs

In a large bowl, combine white wine, lemon juice, orange juice, sugar and milk. Whisk until well combined. Transfer mixture to a freezer container and place in freezer until solid. To serve, scoop sherbet into tall glasses or bowls and garnish with sprigs of fresh mint.

STRAWBERRIES & WINE

Makes 6 servings

2 pints fresh strawberries, hulled and quartered	¾ C. sugar
	1½ C. white wine, chilled

In a medium bowl, place hulled and quartered strawberries. Sprinkle sugar over strawberries and then pour chilled white wine over all. Cover with plastic wrap and refrigerate for 2 to 3 hours. Before serving, remove strawberries from refrigerator and let sit at room temperature for 15 to 20 minutes. To serve, spoon strawberries evenly into 6 dessert cups and pour wine over berries.

SPARKLING WINE COCKTAIL
Makes 4 servings

1 C. fresh raspberries
1 C. sliced peaches
1 C. fresh blueberries
1 C. seedless green grapes
1 C. sliced plums

1 C. cantaloupe balls
1 C. halved fresh strawberries
1 C. Asti or other sweet white wine, chilled

In a medium glass bowl, combine fresh raspberries, sliced peaches, fresh blueberries, seedless green grapes, sliced plums, cantaloupe balls and halved fresh strawberries. Toss gently and pour chilled white wine over fruit. Chill in refrigerator for about 10 minutes. To serve, scoop fruit mixture into bowls. If desired, the fruit can be divided equally into tall champagne glasses. Pour the chilled wine over fruit in glasses and serve with a spoon.

WINE CUSTARD
Makes 6 servings

2 C. dry white wine	4 eggs
½ C. water	½ C. sugar

In a double boiler over medium high heat, combine white wine, water, unbeaten eggs and sugar. Beat vigorously with a wire whisk, until mixture has thickened. Continue to whisk continuously until custard has thickened to desired consistency. Serve hot or cold.

INDEX

W I N E

W I N E

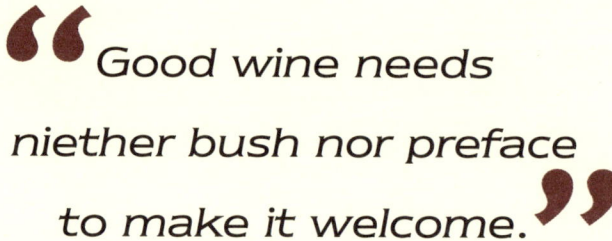

"Good wine needs niether bush nor preface to make it welcome."

Sir Walter Scott